W0017713

FROM OUR TRIBE TO YOURS

A SELF REGARDING JOURNAL
TO CONFIDENCE

THE CLAVIS
COACHING CADRE

FROM OUR TRIBE TO YOURS

A SELF REGARDING JOURNAL TO CONFIDENCE

THE CLAVIS COACHING CADRE

ISBN (Print Edition): 978-1-66784-241-7

© 2022. All rights reserved. No part of this publication may be reproduced, distributed, or transmitted in any form or by any means, including photocopying, recording, or other electronic or mechanical methods, without the prior written permission of the publisher, except in the case of brief quotations embodied in critical reviews and certain other noncommercial uses permitted by copyright law.

DEDICATION

They say that you don't get to choose family, and this is true. In my instance however, my family chooses. We choose each other over and over again in our work, in our play, in our creative spaces, in our tender places.

This book is the product of us choosing each other, and that's why this book is dedicated to Preston, my amazing made-for-me, handsome husband, my love, my partner in all that is wonderfully and sometimes painfully true.

This book is dedicated to Tiger, my beautiful first-born, my son, my midnight schemer and confidant.

This book is dedicated to Devin, my lovely Co-Mama, my shoot-from-the-hip daughter and friend.

This book is dedicated to Eduardo, my creative, sensitive, thoughtful, I-can-shoot-some-damn-pictures bonus son,

Thank you for going on this journey with me; for trusting me in this process, for being willing to open up yourselves not only to me but to each other, and now to the world. You are my tribe. You are my family, and I am so blessed that I get to choose you over and over again. Love and respect do not begin to describe my feelings for you.

FOREWORD

Who would have thought that since the inception of this project, so much would have happened in our world that would shake our confidence in ways that most of us have never encountered or could even imagine? I'm talking about the impact that the COVID-19 pandemic and the murders of Breonna Taylor and George Floyd and so many others by police has had on all of us. And on top of that, the usual stressors of being Black in America. The ongoing, government sanctioned murder and mistreatment of black Americans… our isolated and traumatized children… and the list goes on.

Many of us, myself included, have had to turn inward in ways in which we never have before. Social distancing has caused us to reach outward and inward, and some of us upward, as we have grappled with what many of us now call *uncertain times*. So, with this in mind, and as I revise this book, I am beginning to talk with myself, my family, my clients, and now you, my friends about the following question:

How do we coach ourselves in a way that we remain confident in *uncertain times*?

As you work your way through this book, my friend, please keep that question at the heart of all of your reflections since we are all dealing with *uncertain times* as we are simultaneously dealing with our usual, day to day confidence blockers. To help you move forward not only in this book, but also in your life so that you may tap into your God-given resilience, I offer you these self-coaching questions as a way to begin the practice of giving yourself grace:

- When have I dealt with uncertainty before? What tools, resources, processes, practices helped me navigate those times? How might I use those tools to help me get through these *uncertain times*?

- In whom or what do I currently put my confidence? How will that help me navigate these *uncertain times*?

- How do I treat myself kindly and with compassion so that I may treat others the same during these *uncertain times*?

- Of what do I have control? What do I need to let go of?

- Now, what?

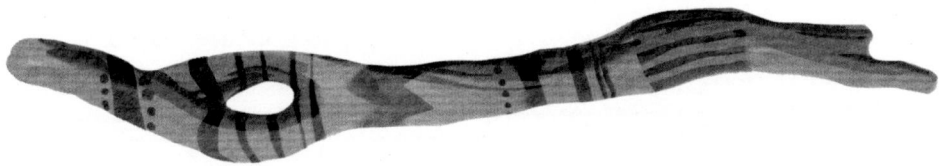

Whenever you are feeling overwhelmed (and remember, we all feel overwhelmed from time to time), reflect on one or all of the above questions. What I mean by that is this: Give yourself permission to sit down, take a few deep breaths, and meditate on these questions. You might even need to write your thoughts down. Give yourself permission to feel whatever it is that you need to feel, whether that is fear, self-doubt, hopelessness, confusion, etc. Acknowledge your feelings and then think about how you really want to feel, and using the above coaching questions, think yourself forward. It's not about making yourself perfect; it's about coaching your self, one step at a time, into greater confidence, greater peace. You may be tired of hearing it, but we are all going to get through these *uncertain times*. Together.

Remember that as in all things, this, too, shall pass, and who knows? Perhaps by the time that this book is published and you're working through the pages with your tribe, we will have moved on to not just new, but "better than before" norms. Let's face it. We, as a world, need to be better so that we can do better by ourselves and by others. And this is a pre-Covid-19 need.

It's all about positive impact and forward motion. With that being said, take a deep breath. Exhale. Let's get movin'!

I AM CONFIDENT OF THIS VERY THING, THAT HE WHO BEGAN A GOOD WORK IN YOU WILL PERFECT IT UNTIL THE DAY OF JESUS CHRIST.

~ Philippians 1:6 MEV

CONFIDENCE. REALLY?

"YOU'RE SUCH A CONFIDENT PERSON!"

"YOU'RE ALWAYS SO CONFIDENT!"

"CHILE, I CAN'T DO THAT. I DON'T HAVE YOUR CONFIDENCE!"

I get it all the time. I'm sure many of you do, too. But, here's the thing: no one is really confident. Not all the time. Confidence, like most attributes, is situational. It waxes and wanes. Ebbs and flows. One can be extremely confident in a particular part of one' s life and simultaneously be totally insecure in another area.

Confidence has to do with belief in one's ability to navigate a situation or complete a task. Therefore, confidence is a shifting, fluid state of mind.

Now, can we boost our confidence? Can we grow confident in more areas of our lives? Absolutely! If I didn't know and I mean REALLY know this, I wouldn't be writing this book. Remember, it's about "belief", and I am confident that if you seriously embark on this journey to boost your confidence; if you will do this work, by the time you have turned the last page of this book, you will be a more confident, powerful, complete version of your current self.

This particular coaching journal is probably unlike any journal or self-help book you've purchased. Why? Because it comes from our tribe, and our tribe believes that real transformation happens when we walk alongside others as we work on ourselves. We believe in the power of shared growth and reflection. We believe that as we make inner shifts, we grow not only in our ability, but the desire to lift each other. Furthermore, research has shown that growth is more purposeful and sustained in the company of invested, honest, caring supporters. At Clavis Coaching^{SM}, we call them our tribe; a carefully selected, close circle of individuals who are about honest, focused, reflective conversation, and who are committed to the same kind of work. Your tribe, in this case, could be your closest friends, or it could simply be a group of people who want to bolster their own and others' confidence. It's important that you choose carefully. The tribe is less about familiarity than it is about accountability.

If you haven't already done so, identify your tribe and give them a call. Get them to invest in your (as well as their own) personal growth by purchasing their own journals. Grow more confident together. The more confident you are, the greater the level of support you will be able to give, receive, and maintain, both individually and collectively.

After you've gotten your tribe to commit to this process, go ahead and choose the date by which you will have purchased individual copies of the *Clavis Coaching Cadre^{SM} Confidence Journal* and have read and reflected on your initial Confidence Story. You might want to discuss the following prior to meeting:

Who are we? After talking this over, your tribe should agree on and name yourselves thusly.

_____

_____

_____

Because we are *(descriptor(s) of tribe members)*

_____

_____

_____

We call ourselves *(name of your tribe)*

_____

Establish **protocols** with and for your tribe. Think about things like

- We will start and end our tribe meetings at the established times.
- All voices will be heard.
- We will suspend judgment.

- Full participation is an expectation.

- We will be honest (with ourselves and each other).

- We will be prepared.

- **Conversations will be confidential!!!**

Our rules of engagement are as follows:

(Add other rules of engagement, as your tribe deems necessary for optimal participation; however, you might want to void too many rules of engagement to prevent making your meetings seats of judgment and conformity.

You might also want to...

- Co-write a mantra or slogan for your tribe

- Create a beginning and/ or ending ritual for your tribe's meetings

- Prepare foods and/ or drinks that are aligned with who you are as a tribe.

- *Example: Sassy Sistuhs* might drink a special Sassafras tea during their meetings! *Bodacious Brothers* might want to create a special Brotherhood brew! Look, this work is a serious matter. But, serious does not mean void of fun!

Where and when will we convene?

Choose dates and locations to meet to discuss reflections on your agreed upon readings as well as your journal entries. For best results, (and because this guide is designed that way) the meetings should be scheduled weekly. However, we know that may not be realistic for all tribes. What is most helpful, though, is to schedule meetings, readings, and subsequent reflections in advance, place them in your calendars, and set those reminders! The more consistent the support, and the stronger the commitment, the more potential for sustainability of growth.

Some tribes might want to schedule all meetings in advance. Others might want to wait until the end of each meeting to determine the next meeting's date and location. Do ya'll!

On this page, place pictures, names, symbols, cell numbers, e-mail addresses, etc. of you and your tribe members as a reminder that you are not alone in this process. Think of it as a *communal connectivity collage.*

FROM OUR TRIBE
TO YOURS

While each member of the Clavis Coaching Cadre[SM] holds a special place in my heart and in my everyday life, (Heck! I'm married to one and gave birth to two of them, and we all work together) and while I could write an epistle on each of them since I know them intimately and love and adore them beyond comprehension, I am intentionally not providing descriptors of them. I believe you will come to know a lot about who they are (or who they were during this process) as you read their reflections. Although we are a tribe, we are a diverse group across age, gender, religious, familial, and cultural experiences. And while each member of our tribe is important to me, what's most important for this shared journey is how you connect with us as you read our reflections. So, I'll just name them.

You will meet **Devin, Eduardo, Preston, Tiger, and Clavis** (That's me!).

Each person's writing and reflective style is as different as each member's confidence story. Each one of us tackled this "confidence" inquiry in the way that was suitable for us, just as we hope you will find what works for you. We struggled with this topic, sometimes individually, sometimes communally. We often had to reach out to each other for supportive conversation. We know that you will have to do this, too!

As the writer of this manual, I took into consideration those practices that seemed to work for all of our tribe members; however, and I cannot emphasize this enough…

YOUR JOURNEY! YOUR PROCESS! Make it work for you! Although you are going to be working on yourself, this is journal is not a 'workbook' in the classical sense. Nobody is going to take up your work and scrutinize it for correctness. Grades will not be given, ya'll! This entire experience is meant to be judgment-free.

From our tribe to yours

Believing we find pieces of ourselves in the stories of others, members of our tribe will be sharing with your tribe, our thoughts and reflections on this thing called *confidence*. There will be two reflections per tribe member. The first one will be their "first draft" thinking about the topic. We call this our *surface* reflection. Each member was asked to do an initial reflection on what they think *confidence* is and how it shows up on their lives. There was no coaching or additional conversation offered during this time.

The second reflection will be the *deep dive*. It will include reflections from coaching conversations and thoughts beyond the *surface* reflection; going deeper, really uncovering for the tribe member (and you) where each believes confidence lives, how it lives, and where it needs to be nurtured.

It is my belief that coaching is more often than not, a side-by-side experience. Therefore, along with the reflections from our tribe members, I will be offering a sort of side-by side coaching experience via some poems, quotes, and coaching questions that will serve to deepen your thinking, especially when you get "thinker's block." Think of these as coaching conversations between us and you as you read, write, and reflect. You'll notice lots of white space and wide margins in this journal. Consider this as an invitation to write around and through text as you're reading and reflecting. The idea in all of this is to keep you moving forward, pushing yourself into not only thinking and talking about your personal growth, but to do the work that will absolutely ensure it. I have full confidence that you will learn from our stories and will, with the help of this guide and your tribe, "coach" yourself into greater confidence.

This journal is a working, living guide. Throughout it, you will be reading, writing, and reflecting upon this thing called "confidence". It is my belief that growth comes out of honest, deep reflection... and a desire to actually grow. You may clarify and revise your reflections as your understanding deepens. That's ok. Do it your way. Now, let me caution you here. There's a great probability that as you converse with your tribe, your thoughts will move from *confidence* to something else. Another topic. Another focus. A mining of old experiences. That's more than OK! The idea is to enter the conversation *through the lens* of confidence (or lack thereof) and to expand the conversation into **what is at the core of your being right now.** What makes you grow? What gives you pause? Why do you feel as you do in this moment?

The only thing in which you need to have confidence right now, dear reader, is that this will be a messy, but rewarding process. Why messy? A client once described her life as a series of highs and lows, mudslides and avalanches. I think that for many of us, this would be a suitable analogy. Building on her description, as we coach ourselves, we must commit to doing the daunting work of digging through the rubble of our lives, and that, my friend, can be messy. Tiresome, frustrating, and indeed, messy!

So, here's the non-negotiable part. Holding back, self-judging, and quitting are not allowed. It takes courage, commitment, honesty, and persistence to dig through the debris of your life. Imagine the work it might take, after finding yourself buried under a mountain of ice or mud with almost no air, no light remaining to sustain you. What do you do? You use what oxygen, energy, grit you have left, and you dig and dig! Now, imagine the feeling of coming out into the light, the fresh air… life! That's the kind of determination, the kind of work you will need to do… unearthing of yourself, throughout and beyond this process and coming out in the fresh air and sunshine of a truer, clearer, more energized version of you!

This study of our own journeys, took us about a year. While we understand that

- growth is intentional and on-going
- each person's path is mapped out according to her needs
- we grow in spurts and trickles

We also know that real transformation takes time and we understand that life, if we're lucky, keeps happening.

This communal-coaching journey of ours did not take place in a confidence-growing vacuum. It happened as we lived. Therefore, we encourage you to see the completion of this self-study as the BEGINNING of your intentional walk toward an improved you. Know that there will be distractions and interruptions along the way. We don't believe in coincidence. Even these events are purposed. Just as our processes, our roadblocks, our ups and downs, were tailor-made for us, yours too, distractions and all, will be designed for you, based upon your needs, experiences, commitment, and resolve to grow and change. We encourage you to write about these life-informing moments, as they are as much a part of your growth as this guide.

After reading and reflecting on each member's stories, you will prepare to share (written reflections, questions, stories, connections, etc.) during your scheduled tribe meetings.

Remember: The deeper and more intentional your reflections, the more you will have to give and to gain! If our reflections aren't *doin' it for ya* at any given moment, please feel free to respond to the quotes, song lyrics, etc. that are embedded within this text. If that doesn't work, do some angry, confused, pissed off writing. But, write! You deserve your full attention and participation, and so does your tribe.

AND Remember when I stated earlier that coaching is a side-by-side venture? On the last page of this book, you will find links coaching tools, podcasts, blogs, and vlogs by our tribe, in which we will not only be discussing our processes as we did this one-year self-study, but where we are in "real time", when it comes to this thing that we call confidence. See how it works? We are right here with you and your tribe, supporting you as you're supporting each other. No worries, right?

Before your first tribe meeting…

Your first reflection is all about you! It is actually several invitations to think about your confidence story. It might seem a bit much at first, but I promise that if you stick with it, you will coach yourself into personal clarity. Try hard not to skip any steps. Try hard not to overthink it. Give yourself this opportunity to really be with you! Think of it as sort of a written meditation. **Ready! Deep breath…Here goes!**

Think about what confidence LOOKS like for you. You may have to think back to the last time you SAW confidence. At what age were you? Was it you or someone else? Can you SEE it? Perhaps you were at the gym and you'd just lifted more pounds than you thought you could? How did that FEEL? Did someone praise your efforts? The way you were looked? What did that praise SOUND like? Do you remember the exact words? Was it after you delivered a speech? Sang a song for a large audience? Tell your "confidence" story. Maybe it was the time you actually opened your mouth and spoke your truth.

Write about it. Set a timer. Write for No less than 10 minutes. If you go over, that's great… but just keep writing. No checking spelling, erasing, striking through, (you can do that later, if you'd like) just non-stop, fluid stream of consciousness writing.

_____

_____

_____

_____

_____

_____

_____

_____

_____

_____

_____

_____

_____

_____

_____

_____

_____

_____

_____

_____

_____

Now, let's explore the flip side. When was the last time your confidence was shaken? Where were you? With whom were you engaging? What did it feel like? What did you say to yourself? To others? How do you feel as you write about it?

As in the previous writing assignment, set a timer. **Write for no less than 10 minutes.**

_____

_____

_____

_____

_____

_____

_____

_____

_____

_____

_____

_____

_____

_____

_____

_____

_____

_____

_____

Dig deeper. Go back and review your two previous reflections. What do they reveal about you? What do they make you wonder? What shapes and shakes your confidence? Why? Now, you're ready to write your *Confidence Story(ies)* or poem(s) on the next blank pages. If you can't fill the pages immediately, take a break and come back to this exercise, later.

Take your first step into this practice of confidence coaching by being prepared to share your thoughts and/ or your writing during your first tribe meeting.

My Confidence Story

_____

_____

_____

_____

_____

_____

_____

_____

_____

_____

_____

_____

_____

_____

_____

_____

Our Collective Confidence Story Begins

After setting up your tribe's protocols and practices, begin a conversation around each tribe member's **Confidence Story**. Write your "take-aways" from your conversation below. Include commonalities, differences, A-has, patterns, new questions, etc.

What you do with these reflections depend upon what you've uncovered about your tribe and what you, as a group, feel your next supportive steps might need to be.

Our Collective Confidence Story

_____

_____

_____

_____

_____

_____

_____

_____

_____

_____

_____

_____

_____

_____

_____

PRESTON'S
SURFACE REFLECTION

I feel most confident when I am in control of my situation. Whether it is finances, business, relationships or my body, I want to control the situation, the circumstances and for the most part the outcome. I am a fixer. I want the problem solved and I have found that when the problem cannot be solved immediately, I start to lose confidence. I've never really needed the approval of a lot of people, but the ones that I do seek approval from are very important to me. Their disapproval, I have found, can be very unsettling initially. However, if *right* is on my side, the effects of their disapproval begins to wane.

I've only recently realized how much my confidence is tied to my finances. I don't know if it is necessarily the money or the security the money represents. I don't necessarily need to have the most expensive, biggest or rarest, but I do like what I like and I do like the security in knowing that I don't have to worry about debit cards declining or checks bouncing. When finances are not tight, in my mind I immediately think, *what does this mean if my family needs something and I can't provide it?* Not being able to fix the problem really shakes my confidence.

However, I do think that some **struggle builds character**. Knowing that you are capable in terms of ingenuity and figuring solutions in times of crisis also gives me confidence. It's confidence with stress, but nevertheless, confidence. It makes me think, "If I can come up with solutions in times of crisis, there's no limit to what I can achieve when things are good."

Like I said before, I'm a fixer. Not being able to handle problems with my family really gets me to doubting myself. *If I had done this differently or if I had made a different decision, I could have been there for my family.* However, not being there for my family bothers me, not being there for my wife is the ultimate slayer of my confidence. I never want to look into her eyes and see disappointment in me.

Short of that, I really don't buy into most confidence shakers. I feel most comfortable when I'm uncomfortable. Doing new things, creating new ventures, and flirting with "falling on my ass" is how I've gained the confidence that I have. Having the woman of my dreams, creating a business out of nothing, and resurrecting my business from the ashes all serve to make me more confident. There are incidents along the way that shine on uncertainty and doubt, but the confidence that it builds in me knowing I will eventually find the solution, is the ultimate victor. It's like those pictures that you have to stare at to see the real image, it's there; you just have to look at it long enough.

Go back and "markup" Preston's reflection. Circle or underline words and phrases that resonate with you or infuriate you or down right confuse you.

Write your current thinking on the following pages.

_____

_____

_____

_____

_____

_____

_____

_____

_____

_____

_____

_____

PRESTON'S DEEP DIVE

In many ways, since my last conversation about confidence, I have had many reasons to become less confident. The business hit it's lowest point ever. I have decreased staff to just Tiger, Devin and myself, my tax situation has hit mass critical stage and many of my employees have gone on to contract positions or found permanent jobs. There are the times when I have my mini pity parties, usually at night around 4-5 am, and of course the times when I feel I can't adequately provide for my family. However, I some how have managed to become more confident and self assured.

I'm not saying that I still don't wrestle with the sinking feeling in the pit of my stomach when I have to go through inventory of how much money is on what card when I need gas or go into the store to purchase necessary items, or when I'm looking at warning lights in my car alerting me that I need necessary service. I still get that, but I think what I have realized is that my confidence previously was based on ignoring situations in my life that at the time needed attention, but I pushed them behind me and moved on. I have been dealing with taxes on and off for most of my life. Sometimes it's ok; sometimes it's not. The business can certainly be a roller coaster ride, doing really well or not so well with the ups and downs. Friends who come and go and when they come they appear to want you to pour into them, never thinking that you may be empty and need them to pour into you. These are all reasons why my confidence should be shattered and less than it was at the beginning of this journey.

Even though my situation has grown critical in just about all aspects of my life, I am, however, in many ways more confident. I became more aware, or should I say I tried to consider the feelings of others when they did not consider me. I extended help to others that I needed. The extension of that help, many times, made my situation worse, even though they walked away better. I realize that the softer sides of me cause me to lose a part that was vital to my destiny and my purpose. I felt that I was confident, and I certainly took a lot of pleasure out of life, but it was always this feeling looming in the background that did not allow me to have real peace. Therefore, I have to ask myself was that real confidence?

Everything still exists from the previous conversation. I still like being in control. My confidence continues to be tied to my financial stability. I feel most confident when I know that I am in a position to take care of my family. None of that has changed.

However, what has changed is the fact that now my family realizes how I suffered in silence. They now help shoulder the problems that I once felt I had to shoulder by myself. I am building a business that will be able to continue to grow and not be so vulnerable to the ups and downs and changes in the market. I am taking permanent steps to fix taxes. I am more present not only in the business, but in my life. At this point I am still taking inventory of what money is on what card, but now I take the time to see the beauty that is life. I see my wife as my life-long partner and not someone I have to protect. My children have grown up to become marvelous human beings. I now know more about my business and business in general than all the years previously. This awakening fuels my confidence. I still have lots of trials ahead to put my life and my business on solid footing. But the steps I'm taking now make me more confident than ever. I now walk around with problems. that could stop many in their tracks, with a smile on my face. Not because I'm crazy, but because I am looking at permanent solutions. I am building on sound principles that now serve me well. Not hiding situations, being honest about money, and working to make my life and my business better by using my efforts rather than the efforts of others gives me confidence.

This process has led me to ask the questions that I avoided. I have always thought I was brutally honest with myself, but as it turns out you can't be brutally honest if you are asking the soft questions.

Brutal honesty.

Let's face it. You can't change that which you aren't willing to acknowledge. With that being established, reflect on the following: In what aspects of your life are you least confident?

Where do you feel you fail or fall the most?

How are you conspirator in your failures?

How does this quote relate to you and your current state of confidence?

_____

_____

_____

_____

_____

_____

_____

_____

_____

_____

_____

_____

_____

_____

_____

_____

_____

_____

_____

_____

_____

_____

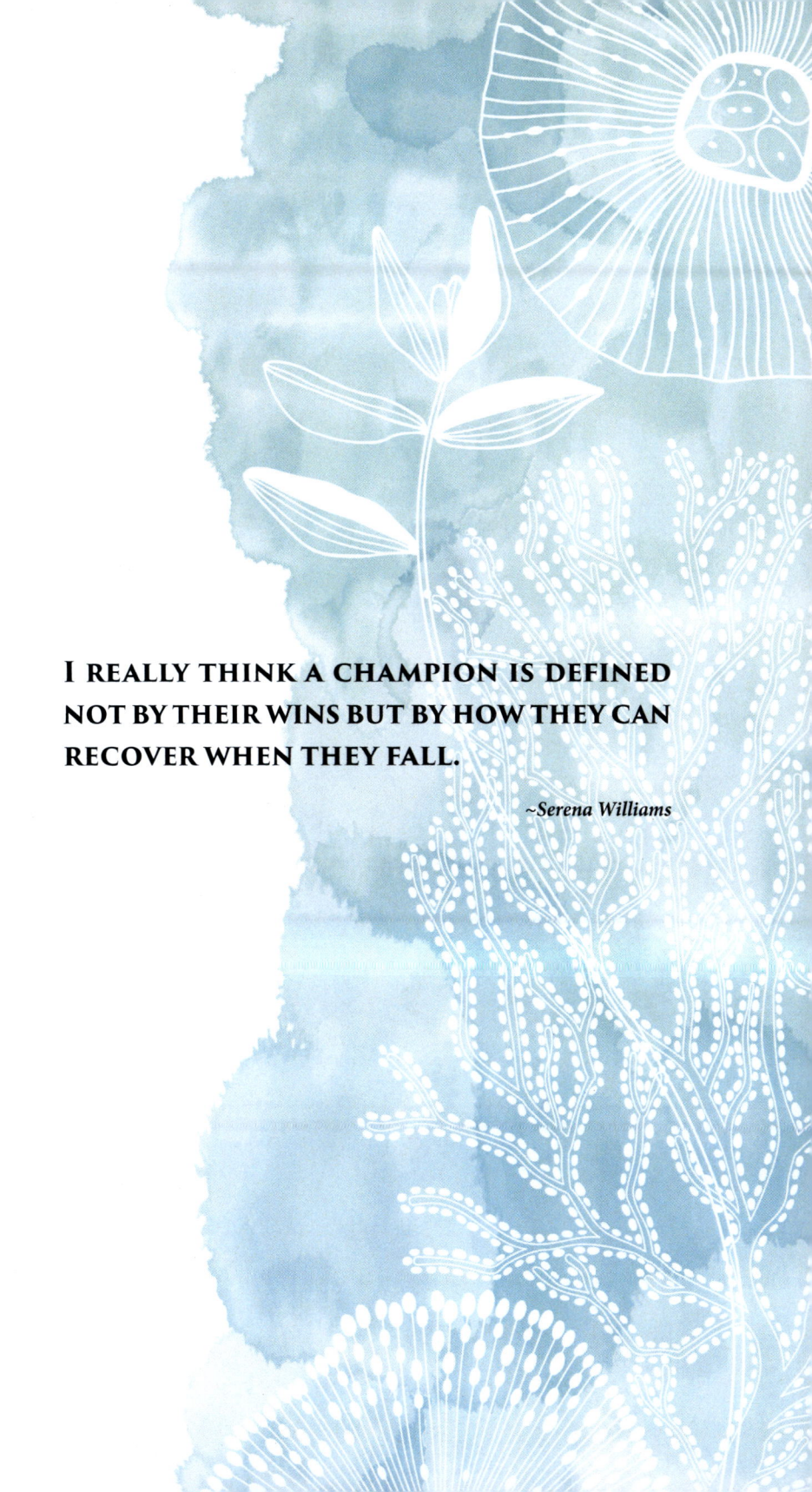

I REALLY THINK A CHAMPION IS DEFINED NOT BY THEIR WINS BUT BY HOW THEY CAN RECOVER WHEN THEY FALL.

~Serena Williams

EDUARDO'S
SURFACE REFLECTION

Most of my experiences with struggling to find confidence have come from some kind of work. Whether it be working to earn an income to support myself financially, working on improving a skill like communication, and/or working to learn and be proficient in a new job role.

I think it's important to note that typically, I am not a confident individual walking into new situations. Over time, I eventually grow into confidence when I've acquired the necessary knowledge and experience to feel comfortable in a role, but it is a painstaking process that involves perseverance. Being a visual person, I imagine myself stuck in a wind tunnel utilizing all of my strength to advance forward through the blasting force to hopefully flip that turbine's switch off at the end. The "blasting force" in this case represents all of my own and others' discouraging speech and beliefs that seek to restrain my progress.

I think a crucial factor in me working towards my confidence is first identifying those unhelpful, negative thoughts/inner self-talk and others' discouraging commentary. I acknowledge it. Realize it is only detrimental to my goals and I begin moving through it. I say through and not around... Or above... Or underneath... because I realize that the best way out is through. No avoidance, no shortcuts. In taking the direct approach, moving through can and will look messy.

You're going to experience relapses where circumstances may just have such an impact on you that it knocks you back to the starting point of that wind tunnel, forcing you to begin again. In times like these, I would be remiss if I didn't mention how crucial it is to have a reliable support system in place to cheer on your efforts and provide opportunities to assist in nurturing that boost in confidence.

Another thing I've recognized in myself is a very stubborn way of operating; I know despite my best intentions, I MAY always have a small inner voice that speaks resistance towards growth due to feeling like I don't deserve something, but as I continue to identify, acknowledge and persist through that opposition, that voice loses its power and grows less audible.

The same holds true for any outside voices (intentional or not) that attempt to derail me. At some point, my trek to grow into confidence through this onslaught of self-sabotage and external discouragement, I have found that it has a way of strengthening not only my resilience but my resolve as well. The "**diamonds were once carbon** that did really well under pressure" quote comes to mind, but that's a bit trite and cheesy. Lol.

Just to kind of summarize: (Sorry it's so lengthy!) I identify my qualms about confidence (usually in a work setting or working towards something). I acknowledge instead of disregarding them. I eventually say to myself (maybe even out loud for emphasis) "This does not serve me", and I attempt to begin moving through everything that doesn't.

When I find myself doubting the process or deeply and negatively affected by something, I simply begin again because "the only way out is through" and if I accept this as true, there really is no other option.

I give gratitude and appreciation to those that truly support me, and that reminds me that I'm not just fighting for me and my own confidence. My loved ones are too, and that's a good feeling.

Eventually, there will come a time when all of my pre-requisites to being confident will be met, (Being knowledgeable, skilled, experienced enough, etc.) and I finally reach the end of that tunnel where I can shut that switch off, and all that is working against my confidence off.

LET GRATITUDE BE THE PILLOW UPON WHICH YOU KNEEL TO SAY YOUR NIGHTLY PRAYER.

- Maya Angelou

Write a gratitude list. For whom and what are you grateful?

How does practicing gratitude strengthen your confidence?

_____

_____

_____

_____

_____

_____

_____

_____

_____

_____

_____

_____

_____

_____

_____

_____

_____

_____

_____

_____

_____

EDUARDO'S DEEP DIVE

Just when you think you know confidence--I mean *really* know it--a new perception of it emerges and takes root. For me, it was the relationship between confidence and faith, but with a very important distinction.

Ironically, the word "confidence" can be found as a synonym for faith. Just for clarity, Webster describes faith as "firm belief in something for which there is no proof" or "complete trust." Out of curiosity, I searched Webster's definition of confidence, and it had this to say: "a feeling or consciousness of one's powers or of reliance on one's circumstances" or "faith or belief that one will act in a right, proper, or effective way."

I bring up the definitions because to me, having an accurate understanding of words is vital due to their power over us. What is imperative to note, however, is that faith generally requires a committed belief in something that may or may not necessarily show its proof. Confidence, from what I'm learning, is derived from actual, lived experiences of big and small achievements. Those, in turn, serve to build and fortify our confidence. We just have to be honest about the outcomes of those experiences and how they've grown us. All too often, we minimize, discredit, or completely disregard life events with seemingly unsuccessful or unsatisfactory outcomes and fail to intentionally investigate how we've grown from them.

Little growth is still growth. Once you decide to acknowledge, appreciate and move through the world with proof of your growing capacity and capabilities; that is when you breathe life into your own confidence.

A little backstory: during my interview with Clavis last year, I discovered that my confidence was debilitated by shame and guilt. She helped me to identify that it didn't originate with me, but were projections of some close family members and friends. I believed that these negative thoughts and feelings I harbored would propel me into an urgent state of self-redefining "for the better" when in actuality, they would only shape me into the kind of "acceptable" version I knew my family/friends wanted me to become... not who Eduardo wanted to become. I compartmentalized so much of myself that I actually began adopting seemingly more "desirable" personality traits and characteristics of other people. I became a fearful, self-preserving imposter that understood very early in life that who I was...was inherently unacceptable. The connection that I couldn't form then was that it was unacceptable... to other people.

Dancing with too much hip movement, effeminate mannerisms and gestures, sensitivity, unabashed displays of emotion, speaking in my voice's natural higher pitch, the slight switch in my walk, snug and form fitting clothing to show the curves of my body, etc. Any of these forms of self-expression other young people took for granted were ways of being that I yearned to have the freedom and permission for. Ways of being that drove me to mental health counselors, suicidal attempts, and psychiatric hospitalizations all between the ages of 14 and 22.

What kind of me would I be if I weren't gay? Considering my environment and the views of my family around homosexuality, would that version of me be a more confident self? Would I still have been sensitive and easily given to my emotions? Would any of the essential aspects of my personality be present? How could I even begin to cultivate confidence with so much interior and exterior judgment happening? Especially when I consider the fact that my sexual orientation was at the core of my self-loathing, but it stemmed feelings of being unattractive, under-educated or stupid, unaccomplished, no sense of identity or direction, etc. My parents once referred to me as their "surprise baby" because I arrived 13 years after my siblings. To me, it's a surprise that I even lived to tell this.

The four walls of my bedroom as a teenager fostered artistic, self-preserving hobbies, activities and exercises that shaped the visual and performing artist that I am today. I poured myself into writing poetry as a creative outlet and oftentimes drew pictures that provided visual representations of what my mental state looked like or the versions of myself I wanted to become. I voiced characters in role playing games and transported myself into their worlds to face the perilous and joyous adventures as if I were really them. I found ways to bolster my confidence in my appearance by taking pictures in different outfits after everyone was asleep late at night with a cheap camera I had purchased with my first job. All of this was my earnest effort to take control of a bleak existence and inject it with as much of my colorful self as possible WHERE possible.

Now that I am 31 years old, I feel as though I have transcended the "it gets better" phase of my past with the space and time to reflect and make connections. One of my favorite excerpts of scripture is in Ecclesiastes 3:1-8 where it states, "for everything, there is a season..." When I look back on those figurative colder seasons of my life, I see clearly now that they burnished a creative resilience out of dispiriting circumstances and paved the foundation for a truly confident self. Now, I can honestly say that I am living in my confidence season.

It is a multi-faceted thing, interwoven with creative resilience and discipline. It is buying into your own inherent value. Sometimes, we get so wrapped up in responsibilities and obligations around us that we may need to be reminded of that value. This is why the necessity of community is ever increasing in my life, but especially as it pertains to a non self-consumed confidence without consideration of others and their support. That is a false confidence. Make it a goal to surround yourself with ones that will remind you of your worth, what you have to offer, your limitless potential. That can provide some of the scaffolding or infrastructure you'll need to maintain confidence.

I know I've talked at great length about this already, but as for me, confidence is remembering where and WHO you come from. When I think of everything my family has endured, embraced, and risen from, it is a rush of adrenaline. I have not been through nearly the worst of what my peoples have been subjected to, but because of everything they have accomplished and represent, here I am. That is the kind of stuff I'm made of, so what legitimate excuse do I have to not elevate myself and others in my community to succeed? Whatever insecurities have a hold on you, disown them. Cut off the parts of yourself that do not serve you and commit to unconditionally loving the fullness of who you truly are because it starts from within. Express yourself boldly and unabashedly as a way of reclaiming lost time. Move through the world with the understanding that when you show up, what you have to offer is significant enough for people to make room for you.

I know that life shouldn't be viewed as a race and there are any number of ways to arrive at a place of confidence within ourselves, but once you get there… once you're operating from abundant self-love and confidence, you actually free yourself up to focus and embrace the work of your purpose.

In his deep dive reflection, Eduardo writes:

"Once you decide to acknowledge, appreciate and move through the world with proof of your growing capacity and capabilities, that is when you breathe life into your own confidence."

With this in mind, list your current *challenges*.

Go back. Next to (or underneath) each challenge, list the *capacities and capabilities* you possess that can help you navigate your *challenges.*

Now, write an action-focused love letter to yourself. What do you see for yourself as you work to overcome these challenges? How will you encourage yourself? Hold yourself accountable? How will confronting these challenges help you grow? Who will you be on the OTHER SIDE of these challenges?

Dear Me,

_____

_____

_____

_____

_____

_____

_____

_____

_____

_____

_____

_____

_____

_____

_____

You deserve more love. Keep writing.

_____

_____

_____

_____

_____

_____

_____

_____

_____

_____

_____

_____

_____

_____

_____

_____

_____

_____

_____

_____

_____

Keep writing.

_____

_____

_____

_____

_____

_____

_____

_____

_____

_____

_____

_____

_____

_____

_____

_____

_____

How do you endure?

What does endurance look, sound, feel like?

What do you gain or lose as you endure?

DEVIN'S
SURFACE REFLECTION

Ok, so this confidence conversation I have been pushing back more and more… Honestly, I've been avoiding it. Reason being, being confident, or rather lacking confidence is hard for me to reflect on, and that all goes to my ego. I know that there are moments where I am fully confident in myself, and those are in the moments when I don't have to think, I'm almost on autopilot, it's second nature. On the opposite end of that, things that push me even a little bit out of my comfort zone tend to shake my confidence. It can be crippling because the fear of looking stupid has kept me from pursuing what could have been incredible opportunities.

So… here goes nothing! *sigh*

First, let's talk about what I think confidence is. Confidence is self-assured, a strong presence/ approach, unwavering, steady, relaxed, prepared. Those are just some keywords that come to mind. I chose those adjectives because that's what I feel when I am most confident.

Am I a confident person? Sometimes.

I have been described as a confident person, but often times I think it's for the wrong reasons. Generally, when people speak on confidence it comes from believing you are somehow fearless, or perfect. I believe that **confidence comes out of those fearful moments**, or missteps. Sometimes, it doesn't even take a job well-done to feel that boost of confidence. I think back on my first audition in New York. I remember feeling like I was the actress they were missing. Is that confidence or arrogance? When I entered the building I saw hundreds of women that were just as beautiful, just as talented, just as driven. It came down to one judge to determine yes or no. As I waited and warmed up and prepared I was confident that I could see this through, but I was also confident that I was not the only talented woman in the room. As

I walked out of the room not getting a callback, getting nothing more than a "thank you… next" it was at that moment that all the confidence in myself was shaken. But why did I let one woman determine how I felt about my own abilities? It took 24-hours and a plane ride home before I realized "girl you did it!" I saw this thing through to the end and I survived. Just a few years prior I had to be dragged to a local audition, but I had just flown to New York alone and seen this thing through to the end. I was not prepared for the emotional rollercoaster I was about to go through but now I know I can do this again and again until I get my yes.

I don't believe that confidence is something that comes naturally. I think at times it can be a front, "fake it 'til you make it" so to speak. Working from a place of fear can and will be your downfall almost always. Yes, we experience pain and fear anytime we try something new, it's what keeps us safe. It also can be what keeps us stagnant, which results in boredom, withering or rotting away, calcification, death.

Confidence… I also think there are levels to it.

I think there is superficial confidence, meaning you draw from looks or belongings. These are the giants that almost always fall. "He will give me whatever I want if I bat my eyes because I'm pretty." Or "I'm rich I can buy my way into any opportunity." What happens when the looks fade, or someone comes along with more money?

Then there is the confidence that comes from the hard work and understanding of your abilities. The artist that poured their heart into their work but knows it's for a very specific audience. Their art may not sell right away but once it does, they may smile big and say, "I told you it was good." The doctor that did everything they could and still lost their patient but wakes up the next day and goes back to work. That kind of confidence takes practice. That kind of confidence takes strength to stand up and say regardless of what anyone else says I have dedicated my life to becoming this person and I won't let this bad outcome shake me. This level of confidence doesn't happen overnight.

Confidence comes from inside. It can't be given to you. Other people can compliment you and stroke your ego, but in my experience the person that constantly needs a pat on the back is the least confident.

So again… Am I confident person? Sometimes.

I am confident on stage. I have trained since I was a girl. I know what to do, and despite the times I've tripped, or my voice cracked, or I forgot a line I was given the tools to keep going beyond that. I am confident as a mother. I wasn't so sure when I first got pregnant, but once I held my baby, I knew I had been preparing for that moment and a whole slew of firsts with every mistake ever made and every lesson learned. I am not confident as a future business owner. It's still so new and there is so much to learn.

But knowledge brings power. Lately, I have not felt confident in the gym, but I'm still gaining control over my body. It's hard and it hurts, and eventually I will get there.

Write about a time when the perfect confluence
of your hard work, your talents or abilities,
and your control yielded "flow" for you? How
did this experience boost your confidence?

_____

_____

_____

_____

_____

_____

_____

_____

_____

_____

_____

_____

_____

_____

_____

_____

DEVIN'S DEEP DIVE

I have had some time since my first reflection on confidence to work on myself and grow. I now have a one year old, am in the beginning stages of establishing my skin and hair care line and am a part of a working and growing community. I have often questioned my worth or validity within my community and that really used to shake my confidence. Now, I don't really care about those things, or rather I don't allow them to skew the bigger picture. I would say to my family quite often that I feel like a burden, to which the response was always simply put, "then don't be." I never understood that until I stopped worrying about what I wasn't doing and started thinking about what I am.

I am the youngest of my immediate family (besides my son), and out of the four of us, I am the only one that didn't graduate from college. For a while, that made me feel like I had nothing to offer in the realm of business decisions and our growth as a whole because I lacked the formal education. One thing I am continuously working on is this: STOP FOCUSING ON WHAT ISN'T THERE!

I am not perfect, so when I'm feeling down, it's easy to throw a pity party and play the "what if "game. What if I had finished college? What if I made more money? What if I worked out more often? What if? What if? WHAT IF?? Those "what ifs" don't matter, they aren't going to produce anything but more questions. I had to start thinking about the I AMs. I am just as smart and capable as any person with a degree. I am a great mother. I am resourceful.

When I started writing out all the things that I am I realized just how much I am worth. That doesn't mean that I can't still grow, but growth takes time.

In my previous reflection the question was asked, am I a confident person? My answer was sometimes. Now my answer is a resounding HELL

YEAH! I know I'm not perfect and I never will be but that doesn't stop me from being a vital working part within my community. That doesn't mean I don't get scared at times, that doesn't even mean I don't question if I am "good enough". All that means is I'm ok with just what I have in the moment. Down the line, I'm sure I will come with more, but as of right now what you see is what you get. There isn't anymore hiding.

This deep dive, like my previous reflection, took a lot of time, but it wasn't because I was fearful, or that the topic at hand was a sore spot. I needed the time to truly reflect on how I have changed. How has life affected me and my confidence? I had to look in the mirror and truly see who I am now. I had to see me for me. Not for who I thought I wanted to be or was supposed to be. Not who anyone else might have thought I was. I had to see who I am at current. When it comes to confidence, it's important to start at the core of who you are. What are your morals? What are your flaws? What are your quirks? How do all the many little things shape you? And how does that affect the way that you move? For example, I used to tell people that I was shy because when I walk into a room with other people I don't automatically engage. Then I realized I am very selective with who I choose to be in my space and energy. I have to be. I am an extreme empath, so I have to be protective of my space. I'm not shy, I'm an introvert. Now I don't have to feel bad or make excuses for not engaging. I can state, without feeling guilty, "that type of energy is not welcome in my space right now." That's just one example of how I came to grips with who and what I am.

When I silenced the other people, and the "what ifs", I was able to have a conversation with myself. Within that conversation, I started to find me. That conversation is ongoing and ever- changing. As I grow and develop in my almost 30s, not only can I see who I am, I'm now clearly able to see who I want to become.

I recently started gardening with my mom, and what I'm learning is that people are a lot like plants. I used to think that plants just needed sunlight and water and either they grow or they die. I didn't know that if a plant started to die you could treat it and it start to grow again. Well, people are the same way. When we become stagnant, like a plant, you start to die. It's time to be repotted or fertilized. When I feel stagnant, I look at myself and think what can I do right now? Not what can I do in a few days if I buy a, b, and c. What can I do right now, in this moment, to stimulate growth? Then I think about what can be done in the next few days, weeks, years.

Confidence doesn't have to be shaken or even ever changing. I now think confidence is being fine with who you are and what you have in this instant. Once I started to master that, I realized that I am a very confident person, because if I can't live with myself right now in this instant I can't expect anyone else to. When I step out into the world, what you see is what you get. Take it or leave it. But either way, I will be fine because I will be standing proudly in my truth.

Devin writes: "I will be fine because I will be standing proudly in my truth."

Take a moment to stand proudly in your truth. You may need to look back through past reflections or talk with tribe/ family members who can assist you in unpacking your truth. Your truth is neither beautiful nor ugly. Your truth is YOURS. It shapes, supports, validates, and illuminates your strengths and possibilities.

I stand proudly in my truth when…

TIGER'S
SURFACE REFLECTION

I've always been said to be considered a "very confident" person. And I think I get what that means. It's an assessment of how people perceive I move through the world with **a belief in myself**. And the *ways* I'm confident in myself and the things in which I'm most confident would certainly lead people to think that. I've always been most consistently confident in my ability to think and in the resilience of my body. Those have been the primary ways that I've been able to affect change around me and make an impression on my environment, and they make up the primary interface between me and the world and other people. I haven't always been confident in my looks or even in my ability to sing. But I'm fast, strong, and resilient both in body and in mind. I think this is why I have a near irrational fear of head trauma and am also very frustrated anytime I get sick.

The idea of a wholly confident person, however, I just think is a bit of a misnomer. I don't even think I know what that means. Perhaps it means that most of the areas that I consider for levels of confidence are, overall, more full than not...I don't know. I think of confidence as a sort of faith. There are parts of myself, internal resources, that I just "believe" in... and there are always things that can shake that belief. And then there are certain ones of those aspects that can be more quickly shaken than others. I, however, consider myself as having lower confidence when it gets shaken and I'm not able to recover my faith in that part of myself quickly. My intellect almost never takes this kind of hit. There are things that I feel I could grasp, eventually, but don't have the will to really try; quantum physics. But if there is something that I can't quickly grasp, like trying to nuke this final bit of belly fat, I'm actually more inspired to overcome this mental obstacle; and I'm always sure that my mind will instruct my body on just what it needs to do to succeed. Success, then isn't a matter of probability, but a predetermined fact.

So, confidence, for me is a multi-layered reality for me that would call me to interrogate various aspects of myself and how this even means I view myself, my composition, and how I decide in what I put my faith and how much of a "faith" reservoir I need for that particular aspect.

What experiences fill your "faith" reservoir?

_____

_____

_____

_____

_____

_____

_____

_____

_____

_____

_____

_____

_____

_____

_____

TIGER'S DEEP DIVE

In my initial reflection, I remember writing that I believed confidence to be a kind of faith. I, however, don't define faith as non-evidentiary. I absolutely, believe that faith requires evidence. Confidence is a narrative believed in that allows a person to move, but it is born out of a lineage of "wins". And when I say a win, I mean anything from achieving the highest levels of success to just surviving a thing; either way, completing or seeing a thing all the way through. Confidence looks at the past and gives you the wherewithal to move forward into the less familiar. You enter into a situation that you have not been in before, but within in you know that you feel some of what you've felt before activating inside of you in a way that makes you know that you can accomplish what must be accomplished. While the situation is new, you still feel that you know some of what to expect, and the unfamiliar terrain is an opportunity to expand one's capabilities and grow one's capacity.

I've been thinking about how confidence is constructed. I think that, for me, it comes out of the fact that my parents protected me and gave me everything I needed and much of what I wanted. Food, enjoyment, emotional support…they all "happened". So, I developed a confidence in them that I was, in many ways, able to take for granted. I knew that I'd be provided for, so I was able to be self- concerned. My surroundings were certain, so I could focus on garnering the experiences necessary to shore up my belief in my own experiences. Even as a young adult, painfully losing a job, my first painful break up, staying in a different city than my parents, working several kinds of jobs, getting apartments, etc. all helped me realize just how capable I am at both surviving and making things happen.

This year has been different, though. I have been, and am being, tested. I'm no longer able to be just concerned about my own survival. I have to be concerned about my family's prosperity. Whereas my surroundings were always certain, I am now becoming responsible for helping make sure that the environments we create are still stable and certain. And in this, I am growing in any number of ways.

Thinking about confidence in this way, however, has left me with so many questions. In my model of confidence, I spatialize the various aspects of myself in which I have confidence by metaphorically representing them as reservoirs. So now I wonder, as confidence grows, so too do the reservoirs…or are they of fixed capacity, and you just operate within them at higher levels. Are they infinitely profound? I don't know the answer to this, and I'm not sure that it is important to. I also wonder if it is enough.

What does confidence need as a sort of "dream team" of traits to help garner the best chances of success?

What does confidence say about self-value and self esteem…and what happens when confidence is tied to the state of things external to you, like your financial situation? Should confidence be tied to anything other than one's sense of self?

And in a world where certain people are always told to be hard, strong, resilient…and are never allowed to express vulnerability, lest they be exposed to danger, should we be trying to build up incontrovertible confidence? Is vulnerability a lack in just strength and resources, a lack in confidence… both? I'm sure I'll be pondering on these things over this next year, in particular. Should confidence be tied to anything other than one's sense of self?

Respond and discuss with your tribe the following...

Is vulnerability a lack in just strength and resources, a lack in confidence...both?

_____

_____

_____

_____

_____

_____

_____

_____

Should confidence be tied to anything other than one's sense of self?

_____

_____

_____

_____

_____

_____

_____

_____

_____

CLAVIS'S
SURFACE REFLECTION

It is no surprise to me that as I am talking about confidence with people and coaching my tribe into increasing their confidence and writing a book about confidence that my confidence comes under attack. Being who I am, I believe that there is no such thing as coincidence and that those things you think upon are prayers that come from inside you, illuminating a need that perhaps you aren't even conscious of, and that the universe is so friendly and responsive to your needs that what it is that you really need, manifests. There is something I am supposed to learn about myself right now. Something about my own confidence. So, I am stopping here to coach myself.

Here's my truth. My confidence is waning, and it's because over the past few weeks, there have been issues with my business. Some companies have taken credit for the work that I've done in schools and districts. There have been issues with finances. Issues with commitment to the business relationships we have established. One client even stated, "I don't know if I can afford Clavis." This really gets me steamed. Why? For several reasons. This particular school can't afford **not to use** our services. They have been and still are failing. Teacher dissatisfaction runs rampant in this school. Furthermore, according to data, the limited coaching work that we have done in this particular school has been more beneficial and has had a greater impact on improving instruction than the more expensive "programs" that the client somehow can afford.

And I've experienced betrayal. Personal and professional. Groups of people have gotten together and literally lied about what I do and how I do it, causing me to lose a major contract.

Sounds like I'm angry? Sounds like I'm taking it personally? Damn right!

I have an ego like everyone else. Not out of control. But, I do have an ego. I have feelings… strong feelings about the quality of the work we are doing in schools. We work hard to build and maintain relationships, especially with and between student and teachers. A program can't do that! I see the exponential growth that takes place… mindset shifts. Changes in practices and attitudes (both adults and students) … that a program can't broker.

So, is this about me? Yes! I invest intellectually and emotionally in the schools I serve. I'm not doing this work just to get paid. I believe in doing meaningful work, especially in schools in which students and teachers are looked down upon. Marginalized. Labeled as failures. Like these clients' schools.

Sounds like I'm in my *feels*? Yes, I am. Why? Because Clavis Coaching and Consulting Group© was built out of a strong, ordained desire to provide lift, unlocking potential in persons who exist within communities. In short, I'm not playing. I take my work seriously!

And another thing… my name. The one my mother gave me. The one that describes so much of who I am… is on my business. So, clients who don't seem to take the work as seriously as I do… and who seem not to take CLAVIS seriously? I take that junk personally! It's soul-crushing, confidence draining stuff! And lying? Why lie and scheme? That takes such effort! Why not put energy into doing what is right? I just don't get it! I'm feeling pissed right now, so I'm going to take a break and figure some things out.

LATER

One of the things that I do to maintain and build my personal confidence, is instead of just brooding, I stop and reflect. That's what I just did. Gave myself grace.

What I am beginning to understand (actually, I already knew this, but needed to be reminded) is that I cannot expect everyone to think as I do, even when they say they do. I cannot react to the ways in which other people think or act such that it negatively impacts me. What I also know is that every client will not be a *forever* client. As a matter fact, every client shouldn't be a forever client. Coaching is about release; sometimes gradual and other times immediate. And you know what? One of the first prayers I prayed when starting this business was for God to help me work only with those clients or agencies whose philosophies and core values align with my own or who are ready and willing to change for real. I can't get upset when God answers my prayers, can I?

So, in these few moments of writing my own surface reflection, I have coached myself into feeling more confident. All it took was for me to take a moment to

- **acknowledge** the fact that my confidence felt under attack.

- **reflect** upon what conditions I felt my confidence waning

- **unpack** what I've learned for and from myself

- **recognize** that I've been in this place before

- **identify** lessons learned

- **move on!**

Does this mean that I won't have confidence issues in the future? Uh-uh! Does that mean that I won't ever have strong feelings about these people and events? Nope. I understand that when there is a break in the familiar, there is a grief process, and I give myself permission to go through each stage.

I reminded myself that I've been in this place before. I know what it feels like to lose myself a little bit. BUT, I also know what internal resources I have in my emotional and intellectual toolbox that help me move past this momentary lapse in confidence.

Firstly, I have myself. My creativity, my intellect, my love of questions and the ways in which those have always combined to help me push through hard times.

Secondly, I have my family and close friends who are honest with me and who remind me of my inner strength and resilience. I especially lean on my husband who knows my history. He has witnessed me navigate my way through dark places and come out on the other side, even stronger. He calls on me, especially when I am talking down about myself, to revise my narrative, based upon the strengths I exemplified when facing past confidence- shattering trials. And he holds me accountable, making sure I take the steps I need to take in order to build myself up again.

And then there's my spirituality. My faith in the universe. My divinity reminds me that I have a God-given destiny and calling, and that she who is called is equipped. (Yes, she is!)

I access those tools. I reflect. I meditate. I celebrate every little victory. I learn, **and I return (to myself)**, I recalibrate me, and then… I'm back, baby!

What's in your toolbox? What experiences, beliefs, people, or practices help you to reset when your confidence is out of whack?

_____

_____

_____

_____

_____

_____

_____

_____

_____

Write about your confidence recalibration below.

Meditate.

List and write about how you will commit to accessing your inner tools to grow and sustain your confidence.

Your upcoming tribe meeting should be uplifting
and quite informative. Good luck!

_____

_____

_____

_____

_____

_____

_____

_____

_____

_____

_____

_____

_____

_____

_____

_____

_____

Mother to Son

Well, son, I'll tell you:
Life for me ain't been no
crystal stair.
It's had tacks in it,
And splinters,
And boards torn up,
And places with no carpet on
the floor—
Bare.
But all the time
I'se been a-climbin' on,
And reachin' landin's,
And turnin' corners,
And sometimes goin' in the dark
Where there ain't been no light.
So, boy, don't you turn back.
Don't you set down on the steps.
'Cause you finds it's kinder hard.
Don't you fall now—
For I'se still goin', honey,
I'se still climbin',
And life for me ain't been no
crystal stair.

- Langston Hughes

CLAVIS'S DEEP DIVE

So, remember at the beginning of this book when I told you that this was a year- long self- study for our tribe and that during this year of self-study, reflection and growth, all kinds of things happened? It's important to reiterate that as we lived this process of understanding where and how confidence dwells within each us, our tribe received expert coaching from me, and as I coached each member, and as life happened, I coached myself. I HAD to! AND I struggled with confidence in ways that I thought I never would again. AND (thankfully) life continued to happen.

So, I'm all about transparency, right? Here goes. The process we used to study ourselves was as follows: Each tribe mate was to write his/ her initial "take" on confidence, reflecting on what it means to him/ her and how it shows up (or not) in his/ her life. These were the surface reflections you read at the beginning of the book. I believe in clear demonstrations and leading by example. Therefore, my usual practice would be to share my reflection, or at least write mine first so that I can recall, if need be, for them, some of my challenges, triumphs, revelations, etc. BUT I DIDN'T DO THAT!

I went on to the next layer of reflection, which was videotaped coaching conversations that each person could review to study themselves and use as a springboard into deeper reflection. I believe in clear demonstrations. Did I have anyone coach and videotape me? NOPE! And guess who was the last person to complete her Deep Dive? YUP! Doing it right now.

Look, I have experienced, as everyone does, my share of ups and downs, wins and losses. As I shared earlier in the book, during this year-long self- study, I encountered new struggles in my business that made me question whether or not I wanted to continue. I struggled with my personal life, finances, learning how to support aging parents, spiritual crossroads. There were times I questioned whether or not I was still equipped to be a life coach. As you can tell by my confession in the previous paragraph, the struggle was, as they say, **REAL**! Not with the coaching practices, but with me, the person DOING the coaching. Therefore, I was not as committed and as courageous as I usually am when it came to fully engaging in this process. Why? I was going through a period of confidence flux. Things were changing, and at times, I didn't know whether or not I could keep up with all of the changes and all of the responsibilities and expectations I set for myself as a wife, mother, grandma, entrepreneur… and the roles go on.

I, like most of us, during *normal* times, gained and lost friends and family, and then, on top of that, I, like you, was stymied by the COVID- 19 pandemic and everything it brought with it. Frustrations, questions, confusion and fear, loss or suspension of contracts, and let me not even mention this thing called *social distancing*. I am truly a communal and social being. Therefore, this part really rocked my world, shook my confidence for a while. Reread the previous sentence, please. *"For a while"* is the operative phrase. Right now, I'm actually feeling not only optimistic; but energized and more creative than I've felt for a long time.

Before all of this COVID, I was thinking a lot about who I want to be at the age of 60 and beyond. That has not changed. AS I write this reflection, my 60th birthday is fast approaching, and I look forward to the exciting opportunities the coming years will bring. As they say, I've got places to go, people to meet, lives to change. In short, I've got good work to do, y'all! Therefore, I don't have time to feel sorry for myself and belly- ache about what's not happening right now. What am I doing, instead? Glad you asked!

I am **trusting** what I know to be true for me. Trusting my process; the way I got through the "lost contract" struggle and every other time in which my faith, my confidence was tested. I began by asking myself …

- When have I dealt with uncertainty before? What tools, resources, processes, practices helped me navigate those times? How might I use those tools to help me get through these *uncertain times*?

The loss of my grandparents… when my marriage was on the rocks… loss of relationships…losses in business…transitioning from job to job… starting a new business…writing this book…

- In whom or what do I currently put my confidence? How will that help me navigate these *uncertain times*?

My faith in God and myself and family, especially my tribe … **my creativity and resolve…my ability to reframe, reimagine and get up and DO something.** Leaning on and into each of these inner and outer resources gives me the clarity and courage to continue to live the life I'm destined to live ON purpose and IN purpose. Experience has taught me that if I look outward and inward with honesty and vulnerability, I never stay stuck, and I am unstoppable.

- How do I treat myself kindly and with compassion so that I may treat others the same during these *uncertain times*?

I extend grace to myself. I **take time** to breathe, to NOT think, just to be. **I reflect and talk it out** with myself and with my tribe, **acknowledging ALL of my feelings. I am honest** with myself and others about my capacity to deal with said situation and expect that they will understand. I **go for walks or exercise.** I spend unencumbered, quality time with my tribe. I set boundaries. I plant stuff. I read and **practice gratitude.** I take long, relaxing spiritual baths. **I pray.** I meditate. I remind myself from whence I've come and of the responsibility to my ancestors. And I work on myself. Why? Because of the next part…

- Of what do I have control? What do I need to let go of?

I honestly acknowledge that of which I have no control by saying, *"God, that part is in your hands. I can't control the Corona virus and its global impact, but I can practice social distancing. I can pray for healing. I can live a positive, healthy existence. I can interact with others virtually. I can begin a new version* *of my business. I can use this time to work ON instead of IN my business. I can write more. Read more. Spend even more quality time with my family. I can complete these doggone books I've been working on for years! I can start the podcast I've been putting off doing, **and I can continue to put complete faith in who I am and whose I am as I do the work I am called to do.***"

- Now, what?

What has remained unshakeable is my belief in my resolve. I have always known that no matter how hard or long the rise, I would get up. Staying down or counting myself out has never been an option for me. My resolve. That's at the core of my confidence; that and the fact that I am a consummate student. Everything that happens in my life turns into a lesson for me, and as long as I can learn something from a situation, I'm good!

So, I'll do what I always do. I'll go to work! That's what I'm doing right now. I'm completing this book and preparing it for publishing. I'm literally *feeling* renewed confidence as I type these words. I can feel it in my body, almost at the cellular level. I am actually grinning right now! I can hardly wait to see what comes next!

Now, it's your turn. Try on my self-coaching process. Think about a place in your life in which you're still stuck or struggling. Is it a toxic relationship? Problems with parental or in-law boundaries? Transitioning to a new job? Aging? Body image?

_____

_____

_____

_____

_____

_____

_____

_____

_____

_____

_____

_____

_____

_____

_____

_____

_____

_____

_____

_____

_____

_____

_____

_____

_____

To aid your reflective process, visit our website,

https://www.claviscoachingandconsulting.com.

Underneath the *Freebies* tab, locate the *Locus of Control* (LOC) document. Read it. Print and fill it out the worksheet as outlined. You might want to paste it your journal, on your mirror, or next to where you meditate. The idea is to release yourself from worrying about things over which you have no control. Power comes in taking control where possible and letting go of those things over which we have no control.

Be prepared to share your reflections and next steps in your next tribe meeting.

FROM OUR TRIBE
TO YOURS

We are a family; a tribe that honestly believes in open, thoughtful communication. We believe in the power of sitting knee-to knee, eye-to-eye and really hearing each other, withholding judgment in a way that allows us to grow in the ways in which we need to grow. We give each other grace.

We believe in, probing questions and thoughtful statements that clear the fog that may be blocking your view of your authentic self, and that though given from our best intentions, our questions, ideas, advice can be rejected, and that's ok. We give each other clarity.

We believe that the eyes reveal truth steeped in history and experience, and we believe in silence. Not for the mere purpose of being quiet, but for the purpose of allowing truth to reveal itself in the ways in which each person can recognize it. We can't coach and you can't work on that which has not been acknowledged. We give each other space.

We believe that we are all born with the capacity to heal our own brokenness, and that we are placed in this world to support each other as we traverse life's gifts and glories, ebbs and flows, ups and downs. We have faith in each other.

Although we have not been sitting knee- to knee with you per se, it is our sincerest hope that you felt our love as you read and worked through this guide with people you love, respect, and trust. We hope that you genuinely experienced transformation beyond what you'd imagined; transformation that will leave you a more fulfilled, more focused, more energized, more confident person.

Blessings!